Together Again:

"A Journey through Couples Therapy"

By; Veronica Walter

Together Again.

All rights reserved. No part of this publication may be reproduced, distributed, or transmitted in any form or by any means, including photocopying, recording, or other electronic or mechanical methods, without the prior written permission of the publisher, except in the case of brief quotations embodied in critical reviews and certain other noncommercial uses permitted by copyright law.

Together Again.

Table of contents.

INTRODUCTION

"Together Again: A Journey through Couples Therapy" invites readers to explore the complex web of relationships. We follow the transforming journeys of couples in this thought-provoking investigation as they negotiate the difficulties of their relationships with the help of therapists who are competent at doing so. This book explores the strands of love, communication, and growth through personal experiences and insightful analysis, providing a moving account of the struggles and successes of rekindling connection. Join us on an engaging journey into the core of human connection, where openness and understanding open the door for couples to rediscover both themselves and one another.

Relationship Rekindling: The Importance of Communication

Every relationship relies on communication to maintain, deepen, and reignite the bond between the two people. Effective communication is the cornerstone of all relationships, whether they are friendships, romantic ones, or family ties.

Communication may easily fall by the wayside in the chaos of daily living. But skipping over this important detail might result in miscommunication, animosity, and estrangement between spouses. Therefore, opening the channels of communication once more is frequently the first step in rekindling a relationship.

Talking and listening are both necessary for effective communication. Openly expressing your wants, feelings, and views may foster an environment of sincerity and vulnerability. The capacity to actively listen, comprehend, and affirm your partner's viewpoint is equally crucial. This encourages a feeling of being understood and appreciated, which may rekindle the passion in a relationship.

Regular check-ins and spending quality time together can help stop minor concerns from growing into more serious issues. establishing a secure environment for both parties can communicate without concern for criticism can promote greater emotional connection and intimacy.

Communication can be aided or hampered by technology. While technology provides a variety of channels for staying in touch, it can also result in misunderstandings or less face-to-face connection. Maintaining a successful relationship might depend on striking a balance between online and in-person communication.

It's also crucial to exercise patience and understanding while having difficult talks. It's normal to have disagreements, but how you handle them may make or destroy a relationship. The relationship between spouses can be strengthened by putting less emphasis on "winning" a dispute and more on establishing common ground.

In conclusion, effective communication is the key to every lasting connection. It takes time, consideration, and a dedication to developing your communication skills to rekindle a relationship. You may rejuvenate and improve your relationship with your spouse by actively listening, communicating honestly, and resolving problems with compassion.

How to Handle Conflict in Couples Therapy

In couples therapy, there are many crucial aspects to handling conflict:

1. **Creating a Safe Environment**: Establish a place where both partners feel free to communicate their ideas and emotions in a safe and judgment-free environment.

2. **Active listening**: Encourage each couple to practice active listening, which is paying close attention and refraining from interjecting while the other person speaks.

3. Teach couples how to communicate empathetically by emphasizing their comprehension of one another's viewpoints and emotions.

4. Develop their ability to communicate effectively by encouraging kids to use "I" expressions, refrain

from placing blame, and speak in terms of "we" to promote togetherness.

5. **Identify Triggers and Patterns**: Assist the couple in identifying communication patterns that may result in misconceptions as well as conflict-causing triggers.

6. **Teach Conflict Resolution Techniques**: To assist couples in resolving disputes, teach strategies including compromise, bargaining, and finding win-win solutions.

7. Encourage partners to affirm and acknowledge each other's emotions and experiences to foster a feeling of emotional support.

8. **Manage Emotions**: Use relaxation techniques or mindfulness to aid in controlling strong emotions during debates, such as anger or irritation.

9. **Discover Underlying difficulties**: Assist the couple in looking into any difficulties or experiences from the past that could be affecting their current disputes.

Together Again.

10. Assign activities to partners as homework so they may practice communication and conflict resolution outside of therapy sessions.

11. Time management: Allocate enough time to discuss each partner's issues and make sure they each get an opportunity to speak.

12. Act as a mediator to encourage fruitful dialogues, ensuring that all parties have an opportunity to speak and be heard.

13. Focus on Solutions: Encourage the couple to work cooperatively to discover solutions as opposed to blaming each other.

14. Manage Escalation: Teach de-escalation strategies, such as taking pauses when emotions are high, to stop disputes from getting out of hand.

15. Celebrate Progress: Recognize and applaud the couple's accomplishments in strengthening their communication and conflict-resolution skills, no matter how little those steps may be.

Keep in mind that every couple is different, and the strategy may change depending on their particular dynamics and demands. It's

critical to customize your interventions to the needs of the relationship.

Rebuilding Trust and Intimacy

It takes time and effort to reestablish trust and closeness in a relationship. Here are some actions to think about:

1. **Honest and Open Communication**: To begin, have frank discussions regarding the events that caused the trust to be betrayed. Encourage your spouse to express their feelings, ideas, and worries by doing the same.

2. **Accept Responsibility**: Recognize your part in the erosion of trust and accept accountability for your deeds. Show honest regret and apologize profusely.

3. **Consistency:** Act in a way that is consistent with what you say. Over time, building trust requires a series of constructive activities.

Together Again.

4. **Transparency**: Be forthright in discussing your choices and activities. Share pertinent facts voluntarily to promote openness and trust-building.

5. **Set Boundaries**: Agree on some definite boundaries with your relationship. Respecting these limitations will contribute to the creation of a respectful and safe environment for trust-building.

6. **Forgiveness** : If your partner is the one who betrayed your trust, try practicing forgiveness when the time is right. Rebuilding might be hampered by harboring bitterness.

7. **Seek Professional Assistance**: Take into account psychotherapy or marital therapy. A qualified expert can help you through the procedure and offer advice that is specific to your relationship.

8. **Quality Time**: Spending quality time together will foster emotional connection. Take part in enjoyable activities together and converse intelligently.

9. **Be patient**: It takes time to regain trust. Be patient and don't rush the process; let it happen organically.

10. **Learn and Grow**: Take advantage of the event to advance your personal and marital development. Concentrate on growing yourself and strengthening your connection.

Remember that every relationship is different, and there may be several different ways to regain intimacy and trust. Empathy, comprehension, and a sincere desire to see things through are crucial.

Together Again.

Exploring Vulnerability and Emotional Expression in Relationships

For relationships to go deeper, vulnerability and emotional expression must be explored. It fosters closeness and trust when people are honest about their thoughts, anxieties, and concerns. This openness fosters reciprocity, enabling couples to comprehend and support one another better.

Vulnerability, but, may sometimes be difficult. One's desire to communicate feelings in an honest manner may be hampered by fear of criticism, rejection, or misunderstanding. The relationship may suffer as a result of misunderstanding and emotional distance.

Building a secure and accepting workplace is the answer. Partners should communicate empathy, actively listen, and affirm each other's feelings. Developing communication skills facilitates tough talks and fosters understanding between parties.

Together Again.

By encouraging empathy, strengthening emotional ties, and supporting personal development, vulnerability expression has a good effect on interpersonal relationships. It promotes honesty and makes it possible for partners to overcome obstacles as a team.

It's crucial to remember that

Self-Discovery and Personal Growth in the Context of Couples Therapy

In the framework of couples therapy, self-discovery and personal development play vital roles and have a big influence on the dynamics of partnerships. Each person in a relationship adds their particular experiences, convictions, and behavioral patterns to the partnership. Couples therapy offers a secure setting for people to investigate their own identities, needs, and preferences, promoting self-awareness and personal development.

People develop understanding of their prior experiences and how they could affect how they interact with others in a relationship through self-discovery. As couples become more aware of one another's triggers and sensitivities, improved understanding and communication may result. As partners gain more self-awareness, they may share these revelations with one another, fostering compassion and understanding.

In the context of couples therapy, personal growth entails addressing behavioral habits that could be impeding the development of the relationship. This may involve problems with communication, unsolved disputes, and personal anxieties. Partners who concentrate on their own development are better able to respond to obstacles in a positive and healthy way.

In couples therapy, self-awareness and personal development have significant positive impacts. They frequently result in enhanced intimacy, greater communication, and a closer tie between lovers. As people develop individually, they are better able to communicate their needs and wants, which results in a more rewarding and gratifying relationship. Couples counseling may also address personal growth to stop unresolved issues from having a long-term detrimental effect on the partnership.

Within couples therapy, strategies for promoting self-discovery and personal development include:

1. **Individual Reflection**: By encouraging each partner to reflect on themselves, you may assist them discover their own personal assets, limitations, and potential development areas.

2. **Effective Communication**: Teaching couples communication skills that work can encourage frank discussions about each partner's needs, anxieties, and goals.

3. **Examining Childhood effects and prior Experiences**: Examining prior experiences and effects from childhood can reveal present patterns of behavior and help couples decide what to do.

4. **Setting objectives**: Partners may work together to develop objectives for relationship and personal betterment, creating a road map for progress.

5. **Self-care and mindfulness**: Putting self-care first and practicing mindfulness may help with emotional control and overall well-being, which improves the ability to have good interpersonal dynamics.

6. **Conflict resolution techniques:** Being able to resolve problems amicably enables couples to

Together Again.

discuss difficulties without jeopardizing their union.

7. **Professional Advice**: Working with a qualified couples therapist offers a disciplined and encouraging atmosphere for exploring personal development.

In conclusion, self-awareness and development are essential components of couples therapy. They provide people the tools they need to better understand themselves and their partners, which promotes better intimacy, communication, and overall relationship pleasure. Couples may overcome obstacles more skillfully and provide a solider basis for a long-lasting and satisfying relationship by addressing personal growth.

Techniques for Effective Couples Communication Explored in the Book

For couples to remain in a happy and healthy relationship, effective communication is crucial. Here are some methods to improve communication between partners:

1. **Active listening**: is being silent while paying close attention to your partner's words and feelings. Create an open discourse by demonstrating empathy and validating their feelings.

2. **Use "I" Statements**: Instead of blaming or accusing, use "I" Statements to convey your ideas and feelings. Defensiveness is lessened, and comprehension is enhanced.

3. **Avoid Defensiveness**: Keep an open mind to your partner's point of view and refrain from being defensive. This fosters a non-confrontational environment.

Together Again.

4. **Nonverbal Communication**: Pay attention to nonverbal signs such as gestures, tone of voice, and facial expressions. These signs frequently express feelings that words would be unable to express.

5. **Time and location**: When having critical discussions, pick a suitable time and location. Avoid talking about delicate subjects during heated moments.

6. **Remain Calm:** When arguing, keep your composure. If you need to, take breaks to stop arguments from getting out of hand.

7. **Correct Misunderstandings**: If you're not sure about anything your spouse stated, ask for clarification. This demonstrates a desire to comprehend and a reluctance to draw unfounded judgments.

8. **Reflective Responses**: To be sure you understand your companion accurately, repeat back what you heard. This demonstrates your appreciation for their opinions.

9. **Be Solution-Oriented**: Rather of wallowing in the issue, concentrate on finding solutions. Find

mutually beneficial compromises by working together.

10. **Practice empathy**: by imagining yourself in your partner's position and making an effort to comprehend their viewpoint. Deeper emotional connection is fostered by this.

11. **Avoid Mind Reading**: Instead of assuming you know what your spouse is thinking, be open and honest in your communication.

12. **Limit Negative Language:** Try to avoid making any unfavorable remarks or criticism. Instead, voice your issues in a courteous and helpful way.

13. **Keep Distractions Away**: Avoid talking on the phone or watching TV while in a chat. Your lover deserves your undivided attention.

14. **Express admiration:** Regularly show each other your thanks and admiration. Your relationship becomes stronger with encouragement.

15. **Compromise**: Recognize that in any relationship, compromise is necessary. To reach a

compromise, both partners may need to modify their expectations.

Keep in mind that good communication requires patience and practice. Applying these strategies consistently can result in relationships that are better and more meaningful.

Overcoming Challenges

Addressing communication problems, establishing trust, and managing disputes are key to overcoming difficulties in couple therapy and relationships. It's critical to support couples in identifying harmful tendencies, setting up appropriate boundaries, and enhancing emotional closeness.

Couples are assisted by therapists in developing effective problem-solving techniques, cultivating empathy, and improving their capacity to comprehend one another's viewpoints. To overcome these obstacles and create a stronger, more robust relationship, couples must have patience, dedication, and a willingness to adapt.

Step 1: Open Communication and Acknowledgment:
Start by recognizing the difficulties in the relationship and establishing a secure environment for honest dialogue. Encourage both couples to

communicate their wants, worries, and feelings without passing judgment.

Step 2: Recognizing Personal Perspectives:
Aid each partner in understanding both their own thoughts and feelings as well as those of their spouse. This encourages empathy and a greater comprehension of one another's perspectives.

Step 3: Identify Patterns and Triggers:
Work together to identify the destructive patterns and conflict-causing factors. Investigating historical events, influences from childhood, and unsolved issues that contribute to the present concerns may be necessary.

Step 4: Developing Skillful Communication:
Teach and practice excellent communication techniques including "I" statements, active listening, and validation. These abilities are essential for constructively communicating demands and concerns.

Step 5: Conflict Resolution Techniques:
Introduce constructive conflict resolution techniques, such as compromise, negotiation, and finding win-win solutions, and put them into

practice. Stress the necessity of concentrating on the issue rather than criticizing the individual.

Step 6: Establishing Intimacy and Trust:
Set reasonable expectations, encourage vulnerability sharing, and engage the couple in activities that will enhance their emotional bond as you help them regain trust and intimacy.

Step 7: Personal development and self-care:
Encourage your spouse to focus on personal development and self-care. This might entail developing interests outside of the partnership, making personal objectives, and going to therapy or counseling alone.

Step 8: Acceptance and Forgiveness:
Encourage the couple to learn how to forgive one another and let go of the past. This entails realizing the value of setting healthy boundaries as well as the role that forgiveness plays in moving on and healing.

Step 9: Keeping up relationships and further education help the couple come up with continuing relationship maintenance plans, such as frequent check-ins, date evenings, and continuous skill development. To continue learning and

Together Again.

developing, encourage them to look for resources such as books, workshops, or support groups.

Step 10: Honor Your Patience and Progress: Recognize and applaud the couple's accomplishments in overcoming obstacles. Encourage them to be patient and persistent as they continue to work on their relationship by reminding them that healing and growth require time.

Keep in mind that every relationship is different, and their difficulties may differ. Throughout this process, flexibility, sensitivity, and a dedication to change are crucial. It's also crucial to think about getting advice from a qualified therapist or counselor who can offer assistance and knowledge on a professional level.

The Impact of Past Trauma on Present Relationships

Trauma from the past can have a profound effect on relationships now. Whether they occur in infancy or maturity, traumatic events can have an impact on how people establish and sustain relationships. Trauma survivors may have difficulties with communication, vulnerability, emotional closeness, and trust. They may struggle to communicate with their relationships, worry about being abandoned, or become very sensitive to triggers that bring up painful memories.

These consequences might appear in a variety of ways, such as the avoidance of emotional intimacy, exaggerated reactions to perceived dangers, or an increase in controlling behavior. The emotional distance that results from past trauma can also damage the tie between spouses and obstruct good relationship dynamics.

Together Again.

However, there are ways to get beyond the difficulties that prior trauma in relationships poses. Here are some tactics:

1.   **Individual treatment**: Addressing and processing old trauma via therapy may be very beneficial. Therapists can help people comprehend their responses, come up with coping mechanisms, and increase their resilience.

2. **Communication**: It's important to be honest and open with your spouse. By expressing worries, triggers, and limits, partners may better understand and empathize with one another and create a supportive environment.

3. **Building Trust**: It takes time to reestablish trust. Partners who have experienced trauma in the past can progressively feel more safe in their relationship with each other with consistency, openness, and patience.

4.   **Self-Care:** Self-care practices can foster resilience and emotional well-being. Self-care should be prioritized by partners in order to create a more positive relationship dynamic.

Together Again.

5. **Couples counseling**: Attending couples counseling can offer a neutral setting to discuss difficulties, enhance communication, and create plans of action to navigate the impact of trauma together.

Addressing prior trauma may have transforming consequences on relationships. Actively overcoming these difficulties has been shown to build emotional closeness, strengthen friendships, and improve understanding of one another's needs.

Remember that both partners must exercise patience, empathy, and dedication in order to overcome the effects of prior trauma on relationships. Despite the difficulties caused by prior trauma, it is possible to have a satisfying and healthy relationship with the correct assistance and techniques.

Together Again.

The Role of Empathy and Understanding in Successful Couples Therapy

Understanding and empathy are essential components of effective couples counseling. Empathy is the ability to understand and express the emotions of each partner, leading to a stronger emotional bond. Couples may share their feelings freely and without fear of repercussions when their therapists are kind.

On the other side, understanding requires being aware of each partner's viewpoint, values, and wants. Couples are more likely to feel acknowledged and appreciated when they feel understood. This encourages free conversation and less defensiveness during treatment sessions.

In couples therapy, therapists frequently urge spouses to actively listen to one another and create sympathetic relationships. Increased emotional closeness and a stronger sense of connection may result from this. Additionally, when both parties feel understood, they are more likely to collaborate on problem-solving and come up with ideas that will please both parties.

Couples may learn and practice empathy and understanding outside of treatment; they are not merely tools for therapists. These traits may be fostered within a relationship to strengthen communication, foster empathy in dispute resolution, and prevent misunderstandings.

Together Again.

Building Healthy Relationship Patterns: Insights from the Book

Building good relationship patterns requires cooperation from both parties as well as communication, trust, and respect. Here is a detailed instruction:

1. **Self-awareness**: Recognize your own wants, needs, and feelings. You can handle disputes and communicate more effectively if you are aware of them.

2. **Open Communication** : Encourage candid and open dialogue through open communication. Talk frankly about your emotions, worries, and expectations without worrying about being judged.

3. **Active listening** : Actively listen to your spouse by being aware of their words, feelings, and nonverbal signs. This demonstrates your appreciation for their viewpoint and feelings.

Together Again.

4. **Empathy**: is the ability to comprehend your partner's perspective by placing yourself in their shoes. Understanding and emotional connection are encouraged through empathy.

5. **Respect limits**: Establish and uphold individual boundaries. This fosters a feeling of security and demonstrates your respect for one another's independence.

6. **Quality Time**: Spending quality time together will strengthen your relationship. Take part in things that you both find enjoyable and make memories together.

7. **Resolution of disputes**: Disagreements are common. Learn to handle disagreements in a civil and productive manner. Focus on the current problem rather than engaging in personal attacks.

8. **Appreciation and gratitude**: Express your thanks and admiration for your partner's contributions. Gratitude strengthens pleasant emotions and promotes more considerate actions.

9. **Supportive environment**: enabling environment Be one another's biggest supporters.

Encourage your spouse when they face difficulties and support their aspirations.

10. **Forgiveness**: Learn to forgive others and put the past behind you. Over time, harboring resentments can damage a relationship.

11. **Intimacy**: Emotional and physical connection are essential for relationships. Foster your emotional connection by being physically near and sharing a vulnerable moment.

12. **Autonomy**: Despite being a couple, keep in mind that you are still separate people. Keep up your personal hobbies, interests, and relationships.

13. **Compromise**: Find a happy medium while making decisions and creating plans. Power struggles may be avoided and collaboration is encouraged via compromise.

14. **Continuous growth**: Relationships continue to develop. Be willing to develop, learn, and adapt as a team as circumstances change.

Together Again.

15. **Quality over Quantity**: It's more important to spend quality time with someone than quantity of time spent together. Make every second count.

16. **Celebrate successes**: Honor each other's victories, no matter how minor. Sharing each other's happiness deepens your relationship.

17. **Healthy boundaries with outside influence:** Maintaining appropriate boundaries with family, friends, and other external forces that could have an affect on your relationship is important.

18. **Maintain your uniqueness**: Keep in mind that you each have your own hobbies, goals, and selves. Encourage one another personal growth.

19. **Express Love:** Love is shown via regular verbal and physical expression. To last, love must be felt and communicated.

20. **Professional help**: Seek professional assistance if necessary to resolve more complex difficulties in couples therapy or counseling. A specialist can offer advice and development tools.

Together Again.

Keep in mind that developing healthy relationship habits requires time and effort. It is a never-ending process of developing, adapting, and learning together.